HOLIDAY HI...
KWANZAA

by Shantel Gobin

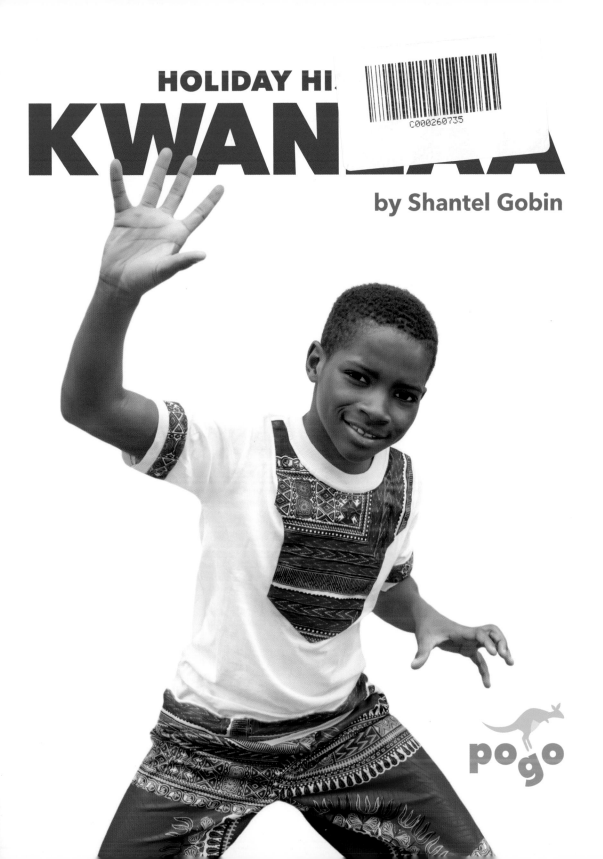

po**g**o

Ideas for Parents and Teachers

Pogo Books let children practice reading informational text while introducing them to nonfiction features such as headings, labels, sidebars, maps, and diagrams, as well as a table of contents, glossary, and index.

Carefully leveled text with a strong photo match offers early fluent readers the support they need to succeed.

Before Reading

- "Walk" through the book and point out the various nonfiction features. Ask the student what purpose each feature serves.
- Look at the glossary together. Read and discuss the words.

Read the Book

- Have the child read the book independently.
- Invite him or her to list questions that arise from reading.

After Reading

- Discuss the child's questions. Talk about how he or she might find answers to those questions.
- Prompt the child to think more. Ask: Kwanzaa celebrates African American culture. Can you name other holidays that celebrate specific cultures?

Pogo Books are published by Jump!
5357 Penn Avenue South
Minneapolis, MN 55419
www.jumplibrary.com

Library of Congress Cataloging-in-Publication Data

Names: Gobin, Shantel, author.
Title: Kwanzaa / by Shantel Gobin.
Description: Minneapolis, MN: Jump!, Inc., [2023]
Series: Holiday history | Includes index.
Audience: Ages 7-10
Identifiers: LCCN 2022023580 (print)
LCCN 2022023581 (ebook)
ISBN 9798885241342 (hardcover)
ISBN 9798885241359 (paperback)
ISBN 9798885241366 (ebook)
Subjects: LCSH: Kwanzaa–Juvenile literature.
African Americans–Social life and customs–
Juvenile literature.
Classification: LCC GT4403 .G63 2023 (print)
LCC GT4403 (ebook)
DDC 394.2612–dc23/eng/20220518
LC record available at https://lccn.loc.gov/2022023580
LC ebook record available at https://lccn.loc.gov/2022023581

Editor: Eliza Leahy
Designer: Molly Ballanger

Photo Credits: MIND AND I/Shutterstock, cover; DiversityStudio/Shutterstock, 1; antibydni/Shutterstock, 3 (candles); elisekurenbina/Shutterstock, 3 (gift); Glasshouse Images/Alamy, 4; Jonathan ORourke/Alamy, 5; selim kaya photography/Shutterstock, 6-7; Hill Street Studios/Getty, 8-9; track5/iStock, 10; lcswart/Shutterstock, 11 (bracelet); Didecs/Shutterstock, 11 (background); AvailableLight/iStock, 12-13; Lisa5201/iStock, 14-15; Dianearbis/Dreamstime, 16-17 (cornbread, collard greens); Shutterstock, 16-17 (soup, rice, background); Martynelson/Dreamstime, 17; SAUL LOEB/AFP/Getty, 18; Laura Chase de Formigny/The Washington Post/Getty, 19; Sue Barr/Image Source/SuperStock, 20-21; JeniFoto/Shutterstock, 23.

Printed in the United States of America at Corporate Graphics in North Mankato, Minnesota.

TABLE OF CONTENTS

CHAPTER 1

A NEW DAY

In the 1950s and 1960s, people fought for **civil rights**. They held **protests**. They wanted to change the unfair ways African Americans were treated. In the United States, African Americans did not have equal rights. African American children could not go to certain schools.

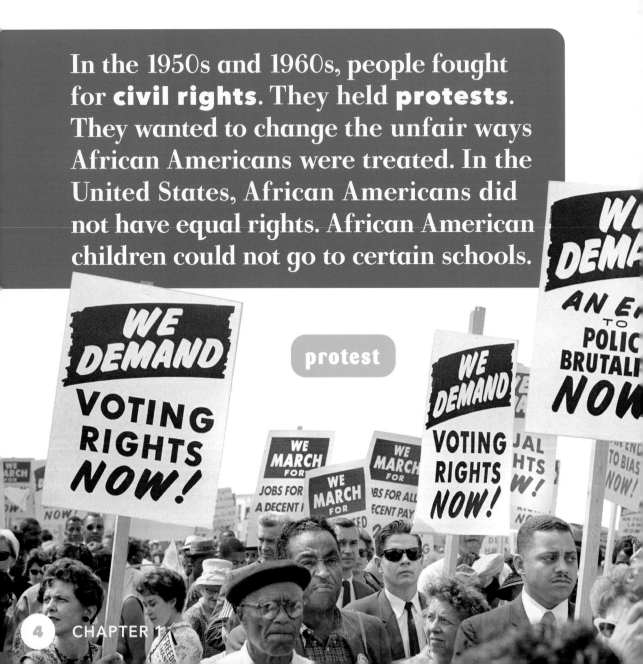

protest

In 1966, Dr. Maulana Karenga created a holiday for African Americans. Why? He wanted African Americans to be celebrated. Other American holidays, like Christmas, do not have a connection to African American **culture**. Dr. Karenga made sure Kwanzaa did!

Dr. Karenga ·····▶

Zulu dancers

The name Kwanzaa comes from a **Swahili** saying. It means "first fruits." People in Africa gather to celebrate the **harvest**. Kwanzaa blends **traditions** from many African cultures, including the Zulu and the Thonga.

The first Kwanzaa lasted from December 26, 1966, to January 1, 1967. It started in Los Angeles, California. Over the years, the holiday spread across the country.

People decorate with the colors black, red, and green. Some use red and green decorations from Christmas!

CHAPTER 2

KWANZAA TRADITIONS

Kwanzaa looks different in every home. But some **symbols** and practices are common. People tell stories. They sing. They drum. They dance.

People give gifts. Books are popular gifts. Other gifts are handmade. These can include quilts and beaded jewelry. These gifts remind African Americans of their culture.

beaded bracelet

African baskets and art decorate tables. The **unity** cup holds water or juice for everyone to drink. The kinara holds seven candles. It sits on a cloth or mat.

unity cup

kinara

TAKE A LOOK!

Black, red, and green are traditional Kwanzaa colors.
What are some other symbols of the holiday? Take a look!

SEVEN CANDLES

CROPS

KINARA

UNITY CUP

MAT

Kwanzaa lasts seven days. On each night, family and friends gather. They light the candles. The black candle is lit on the first day. It stands for the African American people.

TAKE A LOOK!

Each day of Kwanzaa stands for one of seven **principles**.
Take a look!

DAY	PRINCIPLE	MEANING
1	umoja	unity in the family and community
2	kujichagulia	define and speak for yourself
3	ujima	work together and help each other
4	ujamaa	build and support community businesses
5	nia	bring back the community's purpose
6	kuumba	use creativity for future **generations**
7	imani	have faith in the success of the community

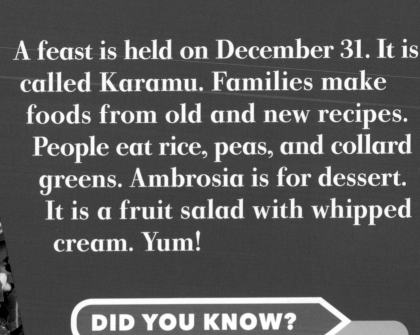

A feast is held on December 31. It is called Karamu. Families make foods from old and new recipes. People eat rice, peas, and collard greens. Ambrosia is for dessert. It is a fruit salad with whipped cream. Yum!

DID YOU KNOW?

The last day of Kwanzaa is January 1. It is the first day of the new year. It is a quiet day to **reflect**.

ambrosia

CHAPTER 3

KWANZAA CELEBRATIONS

Kwanzaa is mostly celebrated in the United States. Many churches and African American museums host events. People gather. They sing and dance. They celebrate together.

People in Canada and the Caribbean celebrate Kwanzaa, too. In Jamaica, people eat jerk chicken. African drums mix with the sounds of **reggae**.

jerk chicken

CHAPTER 3

The message of Kwanzaa is **universal**. This holiday is about community. It is a time to connect and reflect. It is a time to celebrate African American people and culture.

WHAT DO YOU THINK?

Kwanzaa is not a **national holiday** in the United States. Do you think it should be? Why or why not?

QUICK FACTS & TOOLS

KWANZAA PLACE OF ORIGIN

QUICK FACTS

Dates: December 26 to January 1

Year of Origin: 1966

Place of Origin: Los Angeles, California, United States

Common Symbols: crops, corn, mat, unity cup, seven candles, kinara

Foods: rice, peas, ambrosia, collard greens, jerk chicken

Traditions: decorating, candle lighting, learning principles, gift giving

GLOSSARY

civil rights: The individual rights that all members of a democratic society have to freedom and equal treatment under the law.

culture: The ideas, customs, traditions, and way of life of a group of people.

generations: All the people born around the same time.

harvest: The gathering of crops that are ready to eat.

national holiday: A legal holiday established by the central government of a nation.

principles: Basic truths, laws, or beliefs.

protests: Demonstrations or statements against something.

reflect: To think carefully or seriously about something.

reggae: A type of popular music with a strong beat that comes from Jamaica.

Swahili: A Bantu African language.

symbols: Objects or designs that stand for, suggest, or represent something else.

traditions: Customs, ideas, or beliefs that are handed down from one generation to the next.

unity: The quality or state of being one.

universal: Applying to everyone or everything.

INDEX

TO LEARN MORE

Finding more information is as easy as 1, 2, 3.

❶ Go to www.factsurfer.com

❷ Enter "Kwanzaa" into the search box.

❸ Choose your book to see a list of websites.

FACT SURFER